Big Cats

By Dean Iodice

Published by
IO Dice Publishing
3401 NE 82nd Street Suite 350
Doral FL 33122

Big Cats is a part of the Learn About Animals Series of books for young children to get started reading and enjoy the bold colors of the wonderful photos in this book. Dean Iodice is the author and a professional Graphic Designer who has a passion for creative projects. I loved putting this book together, I hope your children love it and experience many hours of joy from it.

BIG CATS

Learn About Animals Series

Dedicated to my little boy Julian, who loves puppies and is at the beginning of his reading adventures.

By Dean Iodice

BIG CATS

TABLE OF CONTENTS

LIONS

Male lions spend their time protecting their cubs. They also protect their homes.

1

2

Female lions are the hunters of the family. They are smaller and faster than males.

3

4

Female lions give birth to 2-3 cubs at a time.

5

6

7

Lions Live in the grasslands of Africa, the lion is the second largest cat in the world.

TIGERS

Tigers are the biggest of all the big cats.

There are more tigers held privately as pets than there are in the wild.

11

12

Tigers have eyes with round pupils, unlike house cats, which have slitted pupils.

13

14

The stripes on each tiger are unique, like human fingerprints.

15

Rare white tigers carry a gene that is only present in around 1 in every 10000 tigers.

16

CHEETAHS

The cheetah is the fastest land animal in the world.

Cheetahs get tired very fast and can only run for a few minutes at a time.

Lions hunt at night but cheetahs hunt during the day.

JAGUARS

The jaguar is the 3rd largest of the big cats after the tiger and the lion.

Jaguar's live in the rainforest,
but they are also found across
other forested areas
and open plains.

23

24

The jaguar stalks and ambushes its prey, often leaping into water or from a tree.

IF YOU LIKED THIS BOOK

YOU'RE GOING TO LOVE
BUGS!

Learn About Animals Series

AVAILABLE NOW AT AMAZON.COM

www.ingramcontent.com/pod-product-compliance
Lightning Source LLC
Chambersburg PA
CBHW060806290526
45792CB00005BA/1542